MUNICH
THE CITY AT A GLAN

GW00537974

HypoVereinsbank HQ
The gleaming cylinders of the
Hochhaus' loom over Arabell;
the expensive villas that surr
See p012

Englischer Garten
Stretching out beside the Isar, this large
park's attractions include the Chinesischer
Turm and Kleinhesseloher See boating pond.
See p033

Maximilianstrasse
Nicknamed 'Pradastrasse', the city's main
shopping street is the focus of high-end
retail as well as exclusive art. Fashion folk
congregate in the pavement cafés.

Friedensengel
From its treetop position on the steep
banks of the river, the gilded Angel of
Peace statue overlooks the city.
Prinzregentenstrasse

Lehel
This well-to-do residential quarter centres
on leafy St-Anna-Platz. To the west is Altstadt,
a warren of streets around the Frauenkirche
that forms the heart of Munich.

Maximilianeum
Friedrich Bürklein's 1874 neo-Renaissance
building dominates east Maximilianstrasse
and houses the Bavarian parliament.
Max-Planck-Strasse 1

Haidhausen
Sought-after homes share this area with the
modernist Gasteig arts centre (Rosenheimer
Strasse 5, T 480 980) and the Jugendstil
swimming hall Müllersches Volksbad
(Rosenheimer Strasse 1).

INTRODUCTION
THE CHANGING FACE OF THE URBAN SCENE

Much of modern Munich is hidden from the casual observer. Behind its classical Florentine facades and austere city blocks lie high-design restaurants and bars, and innovative boutiques. The capital of Bavaria, the largest and richest of Germany's 16 states, is keen to shake off its image as a conservative city of laptop-toting, BMW-driving workers. Such a stereotype can be quickly dispelled by contemporary architectural statements that include its sci-fi football stadium, the Allianz Arena (see p068), or by taking a stroll around the ateliers of edgy, arty Glockenbachviertel. Its style and vivacity give credibility to the local saying that Munich is the most northerly of Italian cities, and there is something akin to a Milanese aura about its 'Pradastrasse', otherwise known as Maximilianstrasse, where fashionistas pack the pavement cafés.

This modern side integrates easily with Munich's traditional past, and swapping Dolce & Gabbana for lederhosen and dirndls is done with enthusiasm. Müncheners can also be proud of their quality of life. The city really works, it is safe, clean and the air is Windolene bright. The Alps, an hour and a half's drive away, provide an enticing backdrop, and several lakes are close enough to be on the urban transport plan. Add in a plethora of cultural attractions, encapsulated by the shrine to contemporary design that is the Pinakothek der Moderne (see p036), and it's no surprise that Munich is often voted the most desirable city to live in Germany.

ESSENTIAL INFO
FACTS, FIGURES AND USEFUL ADDRESSES

TOURIST OFFICE
Munich Tourist Office
Marienplatz 1
T 2339 6500
www.muenchen.de

TRANSPORT
Car hire
Hertz
Level 1
Bahnhofplatz 2
T 7550 2256
www.hertz.com
Taxis
Taxizentrale München
T 21 610
Trains
MVV
T 4142 4344
www.mvv-muenchen.de
Trains run from 4am to 12am during the
week and from 6am to 2am at weekends

EMERGENCY SERVICES
Ambulance
T 112
Fire
T 112
Police
T 110
24-hour pharmacy
Check the rota in pharmacy windows

CONSULATES
British Consulate-General
Möhlstrasse 5
T 211 090
www.ukingermany.fco.gov.uk
US Consulate-General
Königinstrasse 5
T 288 8623
munich.usconsulate.gov

POSTAL SERVICES
Post office
Sattlerstrasse 1
T 01802 3333
Shipping
UPS
T 018 588 2663
www.ups.com

BOOKS
The Blue Rider
by Eckhard Hollmann (Prestel)
**Weimar Surfaces: Urban Visual Culture
in 1920s Germany** by Janet Ward
(University of California Press)

WEBSITES
Architecture
www.muenchenarchitektur.com
Design
www.pinakothek.de
Newspaper
www.spiegel.de/international

EVENTS
Munich Film Festival
www.filmfest-muenchen.de
Open Art
www.openart.biz

COST OF LIVING
**Taxi from Munich Airport
to city centre**
€65
Cappuccino
€3
Packet of cigarettes
€5.50
Daily newspaper
€1.80
Bottle of champagne
€70

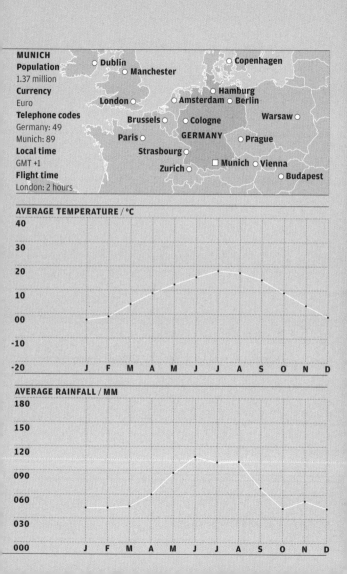

MUNICH
Population
1.37 million
Currency
Euro
Telephone codes
Germany: 49
Munich: 89
Local time
GMT +1
Flight time
London: 2 hours

Dublin
Manchester
Copenhagen
London
Amsterdam
Hamburg
Berlin
Brussels
Cologne
Warsaw
Paris
GERMANY
Prague
Strasbourg
Munich
Vienna
Zurich
Budapest

AVERAGE TEMPERATURE / °C

40
30
20
10
00
-10
-20

J F M A M J J A S O N D

AVERAGE RAINFALL / MM

180
150
120
090
060
030
000

J F M A M J J A S O N D

NEIGHBOURHOODS

THE AREAS YOU NEED TO KNOW AND WHY

To help you navigate the city, we've chosen the most interesting districts (see below and the map inside the back cover) and colour-coded our featured venues, according to their location; those venues that are outside these areas are not coloured.

ALTSTADT/LEHEL

The network of streets surrounding the 15th-century Frauenkirche represent the heart of Munich. The mainly pedestrianised shopping areas, including Maximilianstrasse and its high-end stores, are always packed. Within these few square kilometres, from former royal palace the Residenz (see p034) to the vibrant Viktualienmarkt, it is possible to get a real sense of Munich's variety.

MAXVORSTADT

A sought-after neighbourhood in which to live, partly due to its central location, this area boasts a concentration of culture. To the north are the Kunstareal art district and the university buildings, encompassing the Greek-temple-style architecture on Königsplatz, where open-air concerts are held, and the broad lawns in front of the Pinakothek museum complex (see p036). With the city's main train station to the south, Maxvorstadt is also a transport hub.

GLOCKENBACHVIERTEL

Munich's creative centre is home to many designers and artists' ateliers, as well as the city's gay community, dispelling preconceptions of a conservative Bavarian capital. The roads around Gärtnerplatz are packed with bars, eateries, galleries and one-of-a-kind stores such as the design-led bookshop Soda (see p081). There is little evident gentrification; it's more like a well-kept Hoxton than a Notting Hill.

SCHWABING

From the Olympiapark (see p013) to the Englischer Garten (see p033), this district covers a vast area, its shop-filled streets in the south merging with those of desirable Maxvorstadt. Leopoldstrasse's vibrant nightlife is tempered by classy mansion blocks and examples of Mannerist architecture. Around Wedekindplatz, a rash of new venues and boutique shops have brought a buzz to the neighbourhood.

HAIDHAUSEN

After years of hype, the former village of labourers has found its identity. Now a serious competitor to Schwabing as an in-demand residential area, it is favoured by young bohemian families rather than students. The market square around Wiener Platz, with its food stalls, fashion boutiques and antique shops, is a hotspot, and Hofbräukeller's beer garden (Innere Wiener Strasse 19, T 4599 9250) is one of the city's most popular come summer.

BOGENHAUSEN

The steep flanks of the Isar are home to a beautifully forested swathe of parkland, topped by Friedensengel, the golden Angel of Peace monument. Grand villas, home to Bayern Munich footballers, are typical. The north is dominated by the towers of the relatively newly developed Arabella Park, including HypoVereinsbank HQ (see p012) and the 1960s Sheraton Arabellapark hotel (see p016).

LANDMARKS

THE SHAPE OF THE CITY SKYLINE

By the end of WWII, half of Munich had been destroyed by bombs, but you'd never know, given its reconstruction. It avoided the postwar high-rise blight suffered by so many European cities as they strove to match Manhattan; witness Frankfurt's skyline, for example. In Munich's centre, no buildings are allowed to be higher than the towers of the 15th-century cathedral, the Frauenkirche (Frauenplatz 1), though skyscrapers fringe the city.

The lack of a 'business' district was thought to be an obstacle to attracting new enterprise, until the Messestadt Riem commercial development (see po72) mushroomed in the noughties. Much of Munich's most interesting new architecture has a strong corporate link, dominated by Germany's major car brands. To the west is the Mercedes showroom (see po14), and in the north, the BMW HQ (overleaf), which has been joined by the BMW Welt showcase (see po66) across the road, on the edge of the Olympiapark.

Munich is blessed with many parks and open spaces, and the sheer size of the Englischer Garten (see po33) means it dominates the city. The Olympiapark (Spiridon-Louis-Ring 21, T 30 670), on ground once occupied by the Bavarian army, comes a close second with its superb facilities. But squares and greens are all over town, from the Kunstareal lawns to the Isar's wooded slopes. Müncheners have plenty of opportunities to experience the great outdoors. *For full addresses, see Resources.*

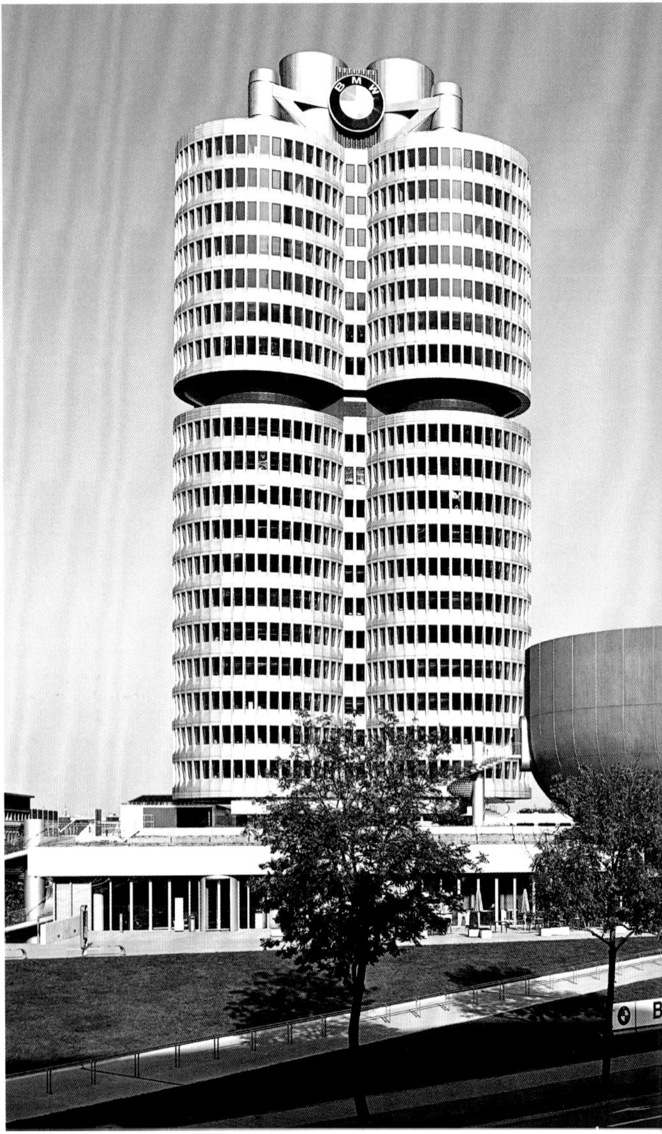

BMW Headquarters

The nerve centre of BMW was designed by the Viennese architect Karl Schwanzer and completed in 1972, in time for the Olympics. The 101m-tall tower was inspired by a four-cylinder car engine, and constructed in a revolutionary way: four large cylinders were suspended from four smaller ones in the centre, before each of its 22 storeys was completed on the ground and then raised up the spine. The space-age shape of Schwanzer's adjacent BMW Museum, nicknamed 'the salad bowl', complements the tower's slim design. The listed structure reopened in 2008 after a four-year refurbishment, the museum effectively interweaves corporate architecture, car design and multimedia exhibits: a guided tour is recommended.
Olympiapark 2, T 0180 211 8822, www.bmw-welt.com

HypoVereinsbank HQ

The luminous silver of this futuristic-looking building, by local practice Betz Architekten, glistens over Arabella Park, from high up on a bank of the Isar. The interior is off limits, which is a shame as Betz's later pyramidal extension has a scrolling light installation by Dan Flavin. The original skyscraper, completed in 1981, comprises three triangular blocks, which 'hang' off four metal-clad service towers, giving it the appearance of a rocket on its launch pad, ready for lift-off. Stroll around to get to grips with the changing perspectives. The facades are free from relief and their lozenge-shaped windows are mirrored, creating a multifaceted reflection.
Arabellastrasse 12

Olympic Tower

Steepling its way skywards, the tower at the Olympiapark is a favourite vantage point for a view over the city to the Alps. At almost 300m tall, it is also a handy point of orientation. Best of all is the kitsch factor of its revolving Restaurant 181 (T 350 948 181). Below lies the Olympiapark, also built for the 1972 Games. Still iconic are the stadiums' sweeping Plexiglas roofs, which were suspended from angled steel spikes by architects Günter Behnisch and Frei Otto. Tours of the site include one for architecture aficionados, while other highlights include the Schwimmhalle (T 0800 796 7960), said to have 'the fastest water in the world', and the Olympiahalle concert venue (T 3067 2414). *Olympiapark, Spiridon-Louis-Ring 21, T 3067 2416, www.olympiapark.de*

Mercedes Building

To make an impact in BMW territory, you have to do something special. Stuttgart-based Mercedes-Benz has done just that with a wall of shiny new cars that tempt drivers crossing a large bridge in front of its building. This glittering, audacious showroom marks the western entrance to the city, and more than 700 vehicles are on display and for sale here. It's no museum, although a few old-timers decorate the in-house eaterie, Daimlers (T 1206 1911). Next to the Maybach area, which has a members-only feel, models revolve or are suspended in a vast atrium. Opposite the elliptic office tower is a spiralling ramp, up which cars are delivered to the six display floors; those facing the bridge are backed by light boxes with changing colours.
Arnulfstrasse 61-71, T 1206 1180, www.muenchen.mercedes-benz.de

HOTELS

WHERE TO STAY AND WHICH ROOMS TO BOOK

The turn of the decade witnessed something of a shake-up across Munich's hotel scene, as the big chains added new properties and chucked out their dated decor. The Klein/Haller-designed Sofitel Bayerpost (see p024) and the renovated rooms by Tassilo Bost at the Sheraton Arabellapark (Arabellastrasse 5, T 92 320) are two examples of this renewed attention to interior detail. At boutique level, the Anna Hotel (see p020) and Cortiina (see p022) are battling it out, with Jochen Dahms' top-floor suites at the former giving it the edge. However, Cortiina's owner, Rudi Kull, does have Louis Hotel (opposite) in his portfolio. Meanwhile, La Maison (see p030) is contributing to the renaissance of Wedekindplatz.

At the super-luxe end of the spectrum, Rocco Forte's third hotel in Germany, The Charles Hotel (Sophienstrasse 28, T 544 5550), was designed by Munich-based Hilmer & Sattler und Albrecht. It overlooks the Alter Botanischer Garten and has a tunnel leading to 30 private apartments, which enjoy a full concierge service. Both the Hotel Königshof (Karlsplatz 25, T 551 360) and the Hotel Vier Jahreszeiten Kempinski (see p026) have undergone recent renovations, the Königshof's by the in-demand Dahms. And on the subject of stylish designs, Belgian art dealer Axel Vervoordt is responsible for the look of sublime gourmet restaurant Garden at the Bayerischer Hof (Promenadeplatz 2-6, T 21 200).

For full addresses and room rates, see Resources.

Louis Hotel

This latest jewel in Rudi Kull and Albert Weinzierl's hospitality and gastronomy crown is situated on lively Viktualienmarkt. The 72-room hotel is accessed via a hidden street in a shopping arcade. Once inside, you feel immediately at peace: the interiors, including the first-floor lounge (above), combine Japanese minimalism with the perfect dose of art deco. Details such as Paris Metro-style tiling and bespoke wardrobes inspired by turn-of-the-century portmanteaus are the icing on the cake. Market Rooms offer views over the stalls and across to the Alps, but book the Louis Room (overleaf) for its 70 square metres and two balconies. The restaurant, Emiko (T 411 190 8111), is the most exciting Japanese eaterie in town. *Viktualienmarkt 6, T 4111 9080, www.louis-hotel.com*

Anna Hotel

Shellac, silver leaf, sparkling stone and soft, mustard-coloured leathers were just some of the delicate materials used by interior designer Jochen Dahms to bring the Anna Hotel to life. The changing colours of a light installation illuminate the excellent ground-floor sushi restaurant, while five top-floor suites bring the room count up to 73. The pick of these is the Tower Suite (above), with a huge bathroom (opposite) that occupies the rounded end of the wedge-shaped floorplan. Room 003 has a similar Alpine view, or opt for the pedestrianised side of the hotel for a quieter night. The super-soft mattresses, informed concierges and complimentary internet access ensure a great stay.

Schützenstrasse 1, T 599 940, www.annahotel.de

Cortiina

By nature a modest man, interior designer Albert Weinzierl is entitled to claim a certain high ground when it comes to Munich hospitality. In addition to all of Rudi Kull's eateries, including Brenner (see p049), Weinzierl is responsible for the bespoke furniture and gorgeously understated details of Kull's Cortiina hotel. On wintry Saturday afternoons, a fine English tea is served beside the rough-stone fireplace in the lounge (above); the space morphs into a sophisticated bar by night, making it the perfect spot for a pre-dinner cocktail. The hotel doubled its number of rooms with a 2007 expansion; opt for privacy in one of the Business Suites, such as Room 110 (opposite). For longer stays, book an apartment across the courtyard, complete with kitchenette and private entrance.
Ledererstrasse 8, T 242 2490, www.cortiina.de

Sofitel Bayerpost

Interior designers Klein/Haller have brought a touch of genius to Munich with the clever makeover of this former post office building. The vast lobby (above) contrasts with a sturdy neoclassical exterior; it's topped by an orange glass roof that produces an added alpenglow to make you look good. The French menu at one of the in-house restaurants, Sophie's Bistro, adds a gourmet flourish.

Enjoy its market-fresh ingredients and, in summer months, daily specialities prepared on the lava stone grill on the terrace. In the Spa Lagune, follow the spiral of the mosaic-lined pool to a grotto-like jacuzzi area. The Duplex Suites have the best views, but the doubles overlooking the courtyard are a better deal.

Bayerstrasse 12, T 599 480,
www.sofitel.com

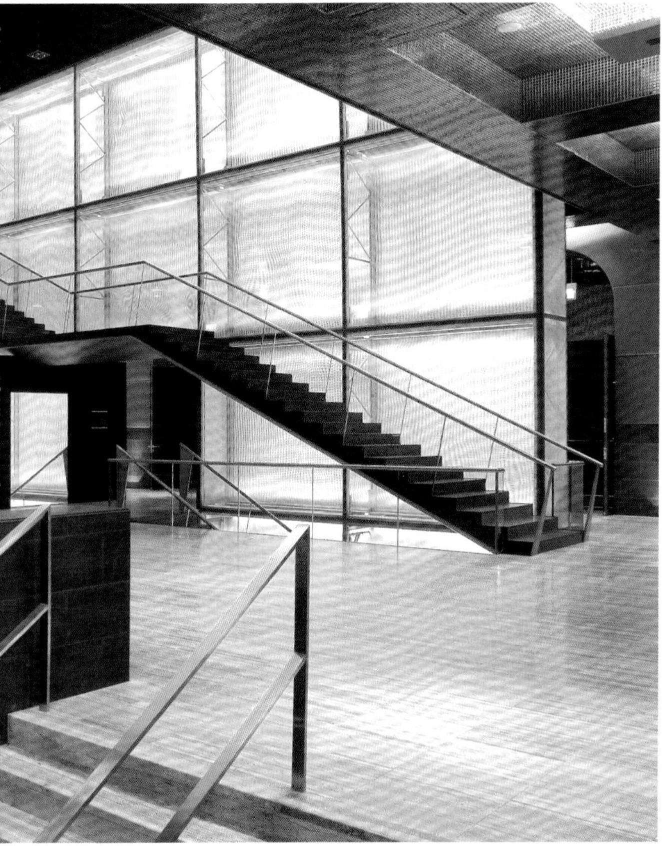

Hotel Vier Jahreszeiten Kempinski
Enjoying one of the finest locations in town, the Vier Jahreszeiten – a cross between a country hotel of yesteryear and a London gentlemen's club – is a flagship property for the Kempinski group. The Jugendstil imagery of the lobby's glass cupola (above), and the bar's wood panelling and green leather chairs, evoke a feeling of privileged grandeur. Since the 2006 renovation of the sixth-floor Kempinski the Spa (T 2125 2155), which features a pool and roof terrace, all the rooms have been modernised. The best are in the historic front part of the hotel, overlooking Maximilianstrasse. The introduction of air-conditioning is a boon. *Maximilianstrasse 17, T 2125 2799, www.kempinski-vierjahreszeiten.de*

Ritzi

Situated on a quiet street running alongside the wooded park that borders the eastern slopes of the Isar, this cracking little local is a quirky place, with each of its 25 rooms individually themed. Part of the charm is the slightly hammy approach: Wayang shadow puppets decorate the walls of the Indonesian Room, the Surf Room is equipped with a surfboard, and the Red Room (above) lets the colour do the talking. The ground-floor art deco-themed restaurant (T 470 1010) and bar are both popular with locals, as is the usually fully booked Sunday brunch, which can attract Munich's celebrities. *Maria-Theresia-Strasse 2a, T 414 240 890, www.hotel-ritzi.de*

H'Otello Advokat B'01

Kevin Voigt's 50-room hotel, more than
a decade old, is as simple and stylish as
ever. Prints decorate comfy, compact
rooms such as the Standard Single
(pictured). With so much on offer on the
hotel's doorstep, the small size of the
rooms is no hindrance on a short break;
book into one to the rear as the tram
on the street side could bother some.
Baaderstrasse 1, T 4583 1200

La Maison

A textural feast greets you at this boutique hotel. Shiny black rococo-styled chairs and metro tiles reflect grey velour sofas and scalloped organza curtains, creating a moody atmosphere in the lobby that extends to the bar and restaurant (above). Throw in a lot of mirrors, canopied booths and a wall decorated with ceiling plaster mouldings and you get the eclectic picture. The 31 guest rooms (104; opposite), endowed with eiderdown covers and old-fashioned headboards, have dark slate bathrooms. If you want some tranquillity, opt for a quieter courtyard room or, for that summer feeling, reserve the Double Light Room, with its bamboo-patterned wallpaper and terrace overlooking the rooftops of this revitalised quarter of northern Munich.

Occamstrasse 24, T 3303 5550,
www.hotel-la-maison.com

24 HOURS

SEE THE BEST OF THE CITY IN JUST ONE DAY

Munich gets the thumbs-up for being a city that is easy to get around. Wide streets and flat terrain provide good lines of sight that make life easier. Bicycles are very much a part of the way of life here, as is the expansive Englischer Garten (opposite), which is where many a Münchener expresses his or her sporty side, although it is also well used for less strenuous activities.

For a relatively small city, Munich punches above its weight culturally and is home to several highly appealing museums, with the Pinakothek der Moderne (see p036) being top of the list. Be sure to soak up the timeless atmosphere at the city's oldest market, the Viktualienmarkt, which is squeezed between the compact Old Town and the grid of streets that makes up Glockenbachviertel. Traditional craftsmanship is thriving in the latter quarter, enabling the visitor to pick up handmade one-off jewellery or clothing that they can be sure no one will have at home.

In just a few hours, it is possible to see enough diversity, be it architectural or cultural, to blow away any preconceptions you may have held about this being a conservative state capital. To complete the Munich experience, there's a compact corner of nightlife in the centre of town around Karlsplatz/Stachus. If you'd rather stick to one venue, start and finish your evening at Heart (see p038), which stays open until 6am at weekends.
For full addresses, see Resources.

10.00 Englischer Garten

To say that the Englischer Garten is the green lung of Munich would be to imply that the city's one and a half million inhabitants live in a polluted environment. Nothing could be further from the truth. Munich is so clean that they even seem to polish the road signs. Nevertheless, the green lawns of this vast park, crisscrossed with gravel paths and fast-flowing streams, are a fabulous attribute. Laid out for Prince Karl Theodor in 1789, the Englischer Garten runs north from the city centre alongside the Isar as it makes its way to the Danube. It contains several beer gardens; one notable, if touristy, example can be found at the Chinesischer Turm (Chinese Tower, above). The park is also a magnet for athletic types. In the winter, when it snows, cross-country skiers glide past.

11.30 Residenz

The galleried arcades of the Residenz, the official home of the rulers of Bavaria from 1508 to 1918, bustle with people flocking to its museums, galleries, theatre and state rooms, of which the Renaissance splendour of the Antiquarium (above) is the most stunning. Outside, the Hofgarten's swept gravel paths and neat box hedges surround the Diana Temple, a Mannerist folly lined with shells. Nearby are the greenhouse-like glass wings of the Bavarian State Chancellery and the shops around the Feldherrnhalle, a loggia most famous for being the site of Hitler's first failed putsch against the Weimar Republic. In summer, picnic on the Hofgarten lawns or seek the shade of its chestnut trees and the restaurant Luigi Tambosi (T 298 322). *Residenzstrasse 1, T 290 671, www.residenz-muenchen.de*

14.00 Alpentraum

Think of a typical Bavarian eaterie and you will probably imagine dark wood, muted colours, hunting trophies and heavy food. Now try again and make it an airy, smart and minimal version with a dash of kitsch and you will get an idea of Alpentraum. The simple wooden tables in the main dining area (above) can seat 30 when placed end to end, an eye catching focal point, but if you don't have that many companions then take a seat on one of the small tables on the other side of the room, or enjoy a cocktail at the bar. The food is a modern interpretation of regional recipes from the Alps, such as venison cooked in wine with cherries. Visit at lunchtime and you will enjoy the same level of quality for fewer euros.
Karlstrasse 10, T 200 030 730,
www.alpentraum.de

15.30 Pinakothek der Moderne
Located in the Kunstareal, Munich's
thriving arts district, this multi-
disciplinary museum is a must for
design lovers. Inside Stephan Braunfels'
2002 building are displays dedicated
to architecture, design, fine art and
graphic art. A return trip to explore
the neighbouring museums is advised.
*Barer Strasse 40, T 2380 5360,
www.pinakothek.de*

21.00 Heart

Don't look for a written sign outside this late-night bar and restaurant, because it only uses a symbol. Once found, though, Heart is everything a night owl desires: a slick one-stop-shop for an evening out. Set in the neo-Renaissance confines of Munich's old stock exchange, it is divided into a dining area with a summer terrace, and a bar that was once the strongroom. Subtle shades of dark grey dominate the restaurant (above), which offers high-end international food, while the bar, perhaps the venue's focal point, has gleaming ochre walls, beige lounge furniture and a mirrored ceiling. DJs and live acts provide the entertainment that makes the long opening hours (until 6am from Thursday to Sunday) pass all too quickly.
Lenbachplatz 2a, T 0160 9090 0224, www.h-e-a-r-t.me

URBAN LIFE

CAFÉS, RESTAURANTS, BARS AND NIGHTCLUBS

Locals refer to Munich as a *Millionendorf*, a village with one million inhabitants, but if it is a village, it's one with some seriously top-end restaurants, such as the slow-food specialist and champion of local produce Blauer Bock (Sebastiansplatz 9, T 4522 2333), and Tantris (see p048), as well as hip bars in beautiful old buildings. Its music and cabaret venues play host to a vibrant scene that veers from rockabilly to punk. The café culture is strong, although nothing can touch a warm evening in a *Biergarten* with a cold stein. In the chill of winter, we recommend ordering some hearty pork and dumplings at one of Munich's traditional wood-panelled *Gaststätten*, such as Kaisergarten (Kaiserstrasse 34, T 3402 0203).

Two of the city's bigger hospitality players are Martin Kolonko of the ROK empire, and Rudi Kull, whose offerings include the Italian-style Brenner (see p049). Kolonko owns the city's best-known club, P1 (see p054), and a number of modern takes on the *Bierkeller*, the pick of which is Wirtshaus in der Au (see p060). Also prominent on the gastro scene are Michael Dietzel – who runs Café am Hochhaus (Mathildenstrasse 12, T 8905 8152) and Bar Corso (Müllerstrasse 51, T 2421 6115) – and Valentina Schunk. The pair's latest projects include the Glockenbach restaurant (see p052) and the Hanoi bar (see p058), opened with Tran Hung Trinh. Wherever you go in Munich, carry cash, as plastic is not widely accepted. *For full addresses, see Resources.*

Gesellschaftsraum

The Bauhaus term 'Gesellschaftsraum' (literally 'community room') is the perfect description of what owner and occasional TV chef Bernd Arold had in mind for his restaurant, which opened in 2008. Superb ingredients are combined and presented in a highly creative way. Expect dishes such as lamb chops with octopus on melon and red radishes, or vodka served in a syringe and mixed in the mouth with an effervescent powder. It's obvious that bearded and tattooed Arold and his staff live the concept: this is an alternative, authentic dining experience. Black 1970s furniture, dark wood and white tablecloths form the canvas for the colourful cuisine. *Augustenstrasse 7, T 5507 7793, www.der-gesellschaftsraum.de*

Edmoses
This refurbished venue is handily situated for drinks prior to a night at P1 (see p054). The space has a goldfish-bowl outlook – three sides are glass – and its interior is bisected by the gold slash of the bar counter, often under siege by well-groomed guests. Sister club, Bob Beaman, opened in Gabelsbergerstrasse in 2011. *Prinzregentenstrasse 2, T 017 7254 7476*

Vinaiolo

Given the oft-repeated local saying that Munich is the most northerly of Italian cities, it's no surprise to find a swathe of *osterias* and the like. Both of the Riva restaurants (T 220 240; T 309 051 808) have a modern and unpretentious vibe, while Osteria Italiana (T 272 0717) offers a more traditional experience. Along the same family-type lines, and our favourite owing to its great food and ambience, is Vinaiolo, located in a former pharmacy across the river in up-and-coming Haidhausen. Antique cabinets display bottles from the Tuscan-heavy wine list, and genial waiters serve up classics, such as pasta, risotto, osso buco and sea bream baked in salt, as well as gossip about which celebrities have recently visited.
Steinstrasse 42, T 4895 0356, www.vinaiolo.de

Eisbach Bar & Küche

Named after the chilly Isar tributary nearby, where the city's surfers get their kicks (see p088), this restaurant has the advantage of being part of the office complex between Maximilianstrasse and the Bavarian parliament. This means there are no residential neighbours, so, on balmy evenings, a 2am finish at an outside table is possible (very rare in Munich). If these are all booked, then the mezzanine booths reached by the spiral staircase are the best bet. Gold, crushed-velvet wall panels soften the effect of the all-glass exterior and concrete pillars in this hip but attitude-free home to politicians and fashionistas alike. The menu includes breakfast bagels, pasta specials at lunch and an international selection at night. *Marstallplatz 3, T 2280 1680, www.eisbach.eu*

Goldene Bar

The name of this listed bar in the Haus der Kunst art gallery (see p062) is inspired by its golden murals, which originate from 1937 when the museum was founded as the first of several monumental Nazi buildings. A vast chandelier that once hung in the Savoy Hotel sparkles above elegant black tables, Eugen Schmidt chairs and the equally sparkly regulars. Co-owner Klaus St Rainer, one of Munich's most gifted bartenders, concocts cocktails from homemade ingredients and a remarkable collection of rare spirits. The bar is an ideal spot for starting your evening and it is also great for lunch, or afternoon tea with homebaked cakes on the terrace. Stop at the nearby bridge to watch surfers riding the Eisbach wave.
Prinzregentenstrasse 1, T 5480 4777, www.goldenebar.de

Tantris

Don't be put off by the location behind the cash-and-carry car park and opposite the police station, Tantris is the city's most celebrated restaurant. The guardian stone dragons outside are an Eastern pointer to the red-and-black lacquered 1970s-style interiors. We love the orange shagpile carpet lining the walls. Several degustation menus are available, with the sublime dishes including the likes of foie gras and soufflé. The wine list is superb, and help is on hand from an expert team of sommeliers led by Rakhshan Zhouleh. In a country where service isn't always up to scratch, Tantris excels. If you have something to celebrate, ask for the limousine pick-up to get your evening started on the right note.
Johann-Fichte-Strasse 7, T 361 9590, www.tantris.de

Brenner

An elite crowd frequents this stylish bar/ restaurant beside the city's opera house and glitzy shopping mile. The original stone arches of a former stable block, some now stacked with wood for the grill, have been encased in glass by Albert Weinzierl. Inside, patrons are greeted by first the bar then the restaurant before the real focal-point: the open cooking stations of the grill. Rack bearing oversized fillets or sizzling rafts of whole calamari span red-hot coals; the new potatoes roasted with rosemary are a particular treat. Either ask for a table near the grill or sit beside the windows for a spot of people watching. In early spring, enjoy the reflected warmth of surrounding buildings over an aperitif in the courtyard.
*Maximilianstrasse 15, T 452 2880,
www.brennergrill.de*

La Baracca

'E-talian' might be the correct term to describe this unusual but pleasing place. Instead of printed menus, the culinary offerings are displayed on touchscreen pads and orders are relayed direct to the kitchen. Diners having several courses should ensure each is ordered separately as the food will be served promptly. The portions, small for Germany, arrive in neat, pretty pans and bowls. The idea is to mix and match. Classic Italian dishes, as well as some innovative creations from Michelin-starred chefs, are complemented by a selection of hard-to-find Italian wines. Despite the high-tech approach, the restaurant has a charming Italianate ambience, aided by the open kitchen, rough wooden ceilings and stone walls. *Maximiliansplatz 9, T 4161 7852, www.labaracca.eu*

Glockenbach
With its prime location and menu spanning
breakfast, lunch, coffee, cakes, dinner and
cocktails, this elegant split-level space is
perfect at any time of the day. The interior
contains a mix of midcentury furniture as
well as contemporary pieces by German
designer Stefan Diez. Stairs link the
bar and café with the fine-dining gallery.
Müllerstrasse 49, T 4524 0622,
www.glockenbach.com

P1

This is the club that everyone loves to hate, probably due to its continued success. A not-so-strict door policy has done nothing to diminish the quality of the supremely glamorous crowd here. During the week, it's chock-full of footballers' wives (and, on occasion, their husbands) along with other faux-tanned beauties. The side-by-side room arrangement somehow works, with the different soundtracks in each avoiding conflict, though if it all becomes too much, guests can retreat to a purple-lit outdoor terrace. A 2010 renovation by Stefan Mauritz replaced the in-house pizzeria with an Asian-inspired outlet. Skip P1 on the weekends, though, when the whole city is trying to get in on the act. *Prinzregentenstrasse 1, T 211 1140, www.p1-club.de*

Röcklplatz

Initially set up by Sandra Forster, Michi Kern and Markus Frankl, Röckplatz was devised to give deprived youths a career opportunity in the restaurant business. Located in up-and-coming Dreimühlenviertel (three-mill district), the organic menu caters for vegetarians and vegans. Interiors by Munich-based Nitzan Cohen pit rough materials, such as pine and raw zinc, against shiny tabletops, elegant chairs and handblown crystal pendulum lamps. Zinc-plated cupboards and large letters dotted with lightbulbs also catch the eye. The garden is perfect on balmy evenings, but to get even closer to nature, grab a picnic from nearby Bavarese (T 5203 3437) and head to the Zum Flaucher *Biergarten* (T 723 2677). *Isartalstrasse 26, T 4521 7129*

Trachtenvogl

This split-level bar/lounge is home to the artisans of Glockenbachviertel, who kick back on the original and slightly tired midcentury furniture. There's no sense of pretentiousness here, just an authentic bonhomie amid the school chairs, retro televisions and antlers on the walls. The open bar arrangement encourages a free flow of conversation among boho guests and staff. It's lively by night and, unusually for Munich, majors on a non-local beer, Astra – all the way from Hamburg. During the day, don't miss the house speciality: creamy, indulgent hot chocolate from Italian company Eraclea. It comes in more than 30 flavour combinations, including banana with meringue, lemon with pine kernels, and orange with cinnamon.
Reichenbachstrasse 47, T 201 5160, www.trachtenvogl.de

L'Osteria Künstlerhaus

When it comes to Munich's many Italian restaurants, L'Osteria Künstlerhaus offers perhaps the most authentic experience, particularly when you consider that it uses fresh ingredients sourced direct from Italy. On hot days, when the huge windows in the listed facade are fully opened, the inside melds with the street-facing terrace and you could be in a Roman piazza. The Venetian room (above), part of the original 1900 neo-Renaissance artists building, with its immense, clear Murano glass chandelier, gaudy murals and mosaics, is a highlight. It contrasts with the more restrained style of the main space, which has an open kitchen and a bar. Another branch has opened on Leopoldstrasse (T 3888 9711).
Lenbachplatz 8, T 9901 9810,
www.losteria.de

Hanoi
Looking like a cross between a 19th-century parlour and a discotheque, Hanoi was designed by Ferrier Interiors, who combined brass wall panels, dark wooden floors and a preponderance of gold colours to great effect. The club has a dancefloor and two lounges, with the funk, soul and house soundtrack kept at conversation-friendly levels.
Theklastrasse 1, www.hanoi-bar.de

Wirtshaus in der Au

Just up from the Isar river, in the Au area of fashionable Haidhausen, this *Wirtshaus* (public house) is the place to experience a full onslaught of fine Bavarian hospitality. Duck breast with super-size dumplings and red cabbage is the order of the day, washed down with a few steins of *Helles*. To finish, try the *Apfelschmarrn*, a Bavarian sliced-pancake with apples, served with cranberries. The staff don *Trachten*, the traditional costume of dirndls or lederhosen, and the vibe is decidedly fun, with tables spilling out on to the wide pavement in summer. In winter, ask for a spot in the alcove by the fire. *Lilienstrasse 51, T 448 1400, www.wirtshausinderau.de*

Zum Goldenen Kalb

The name is a tongue-in-cheek reference to traditional German restaurants and the worship of the Golden Calf. But even without the double meaning it describes what this place is all about: a premium meat experience (vegetarians should stop reading right here). Two meat-maturing cabinets, from which you can chose your cut, are at the heart of this restaurant, whose vintage-style interiors resemble a New York grill crossed with a Parisian brasserie, which makes the oysters and fish on the high-end menu a little less surprising. Raw brick, dark wood and leather create a warm atmosphere, and the white tiles behind the bar are covered in tasteful yet informative illustrations, as if cut from a quaint cookery book.
Utzschneiderstrasse 1, T 2354 2290, www.zum-goldenen-kalb.de

INSIDER'S GUIDE

BENEDIKT SARREITER, WRITER AND EDITOR

At the end of each week, Benedikt Sarreiter, a member of Munich media collective Nansen & Piccard (www.nansenundpiccard.de), unwinds over a whisky sour at Goldene Bar (see p046). Sarreiter, who also writes for the *Süddeutsche Zeitung* daily newspaper, might then head to Pizzeria Grano (Sebastiansplatz 3, T 2326 9939) to snack on 'the best pizza in town' with his colleagues, or to J Bar (Maistrasse 28, T 5146 9983) for sushi. 'Gärtnerplatz in Glockenbachviertel is still Munich's most vibrant area,' he says, referring to bars such as Robinson's (Corneliusstrasse 14), which is owned by skateboarder Robinson Kuhlmann. For live independent music, the venerable Atomic Café (Neuturmstrasse 5, T 228 3054) remains the best venue.

At the weekend, Sarreiter breakfasts on the rooftop terrace at Café Ruffini (Orffstrasse 22-24, T 161 160). Later he might shop for labels, everything from APC to YMC, at the Schwittenberg boutique (Hildegardstrasse 2, T 2601 9055). If friends visit, a trip to the modern art gallery Haus der Kunst (Prinzregentenstrasse 1, T 2112 7113) or the Royal Bavarian pomp of the Residenz (see p034) is a must. 'And for bathing, we'd go to Müllersches Volksbad (Rosenheimer Strasse 1),' he says. 'It's hard to find a more beautiful example of art nouveau.' Wild swimmers, however, might prefer diving into the local lakes of Starnberger See or Ammersee.

For full addresses, see Resources.

ARCHITOUR
A GUIDE TO MUNICH'S ICONIC BUILDINGS

While its northern rivals have been making noises about their architectural achievements, Munich has been quietly building a world-class portfolio. Additions include the Museum Brandhorst (opposite) and the narrow form of what will be the new home of the city's Staatliches Museum Ägyptischer Kunst when it joins the film school (which numbers Wim Wenders among its alumni) on Gabelsbergerstrasse in 2013. Also opening around this time will be Lord Foster's extension to Lenbachhaus (Luisenstrasse 33, T 2333 2000), where art by Munich's Blue Rider group will hang.

The city's architectural heritage is thanks to King Ludwig I and his son Maximilian II, who strove to create 'Athens on the Isar'. Court architect Leo von Klenze designed monumental buildings with classical and Renaissance references concentrated around Königsplatz and the Ludwigstrasse university area. The Residenz (see p034), the former home of the ruling Wittelsbach family, is a melange of styles from Gothic to baroque to neoclassical.

While there is office space waiting to be let, the city's modern architecture thrives. Take the Akademie der Bildenden Künste extension (see p070), the St-Quirin-Platz subway station, with its shell-like glass dome, the Münchener Freiheit tram stop, or the filigree membrane of the tented Office for Waste Disposal (Georg-Brauchle-Ring 29). Yes, public works are taken very seriously here. *For full addresses, see Resources.*

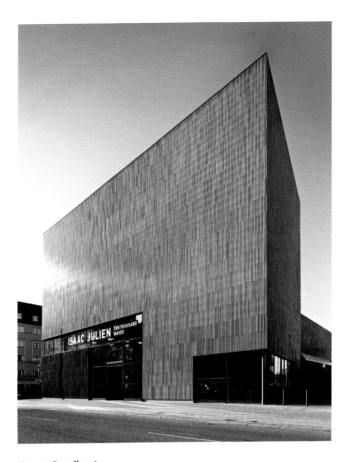

Museum Brandhorst

This modern-art museum, by architects Sauerbruch Hutton, opened in 2009 and houses the 20th- and 21st-century collection of Udo and Anette Brandhorst. Alongside the usual suspects, such as Warhol, Beuys and Hirst, are displayed an intriguing selection of less obvious artists including Sigmar Polke and Alex Katz; notably, the top floor is dedicated to the enormous paintings of Cy Twombly.

The building wears 36,000 ceramic bars that pick up on the colourful facades of the neighbouring turn-of-the-century townhouses. Inside, white walls, oak floors, and the use of leather and natural lighting form a harmonious backdrop. After a visit, queue for ice cream at BallaBeni opposite (T 1891 2943; open in summer only). *Theresienstrasse 35a, T 238 052 286, www.museum-brandhorst.de*

BMW Welt

Part-petrolhead theme park, part-epic showroom, BMW Welt is Bavaria's most-visited attraction. The double-helix of the glass-fronted homage to BMW, completed by Austrian practice Coop Himmelb(l)au in 2007, was inspired by a tornado, and the firm has certainly created a dynamic space. Walkways, overlooking a vast delivery area, link presentation areas and restaurants. In the VIP lounge, cars arrive by lift to a rotating dais, where they are inspected and driven off. With up to 2,000 vehicles being collected monthly, much attention was paid to the energy-saving building's ventilation. If you don't have a BMW waiting, try out the simulator instead. Open daily, except at Christmas.
Olympiapark 1, T 0180 211 8822, www.bmw-welt.com

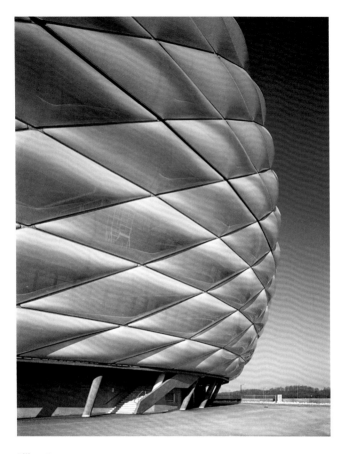

Allianz Arena

Built for the 2006 World Cup and home to both of Munich's football teams, FC Bayern and TSV 1860, the stadium has an inflatable skin; when lit at night, in the home team's colours, it appears to float. The cushion-like diamond surface evokes the Plexiglas panels of the 1972 Olympic Stadium, the city's other iconic sporting structure. Here, with only football on the menu, fans can get up close and personal as there's no running track between them and the grass. Herzog & de Meuron have given every one of the 66,000 seats, arranged in three tiers, an unencumbered view. The Allianz AG VIP box, designed by London-based architects Virgile and Stone, boasts a slick interior that includes a bar, lounge and widescreen televisions. *Werner-Heisenberg-Allee 25, Fröttmaning, T 350 948 350, www.allianz-arena.de*

Herz Jesu Kirche

The glass exterior of the Church of the Sacred Heart is a radical statement for the conservative Catholic church, especially in parochial Bavaria. Local architectural practice Allmann Sattler Wappner finished it in 2000, and soon snapped up several prestigious architecture awards. 'Louvred maple timber walls inside allow light to focus on the altar,' says Amandus Sattler. The church is full of subtle imagery: basement art installations representing the five wounds of Christ on the cross glow eerily through the floor, while the story of the Passion is told in calligraphy composed of nail silhouettes, engraved on the front glass facade. On feast days, the 20-ton steel-and-glass hydraulic doors open over the Jura limestone square. *Lachnerstrasse 8, T 130 6750, www.herzjesu-muenchen.de*

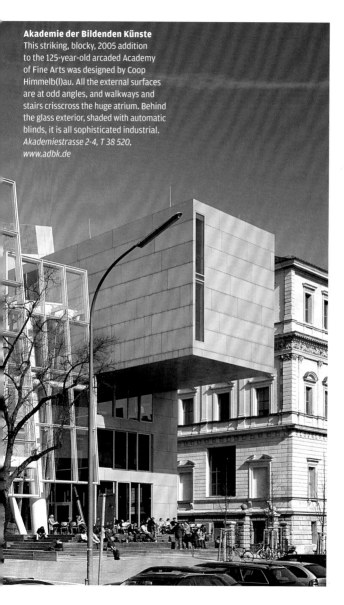

Akademie der Bildenden Künste
This striking, blocky, 2005 addition
to the 125-year-old arcaded Academy
of Fine Arts was designed by Coop
Himmelb(l)au. All the external surfaces
are at odd angles, and walkways and
stairs crisscross the huge atrium. Behind
the glass exterior, shaded with automatic
blinds, it is all sophisticated industrial.
*Akademiestrasse 2-4, T 38 520,
www.adbk.de*

St Florian Kirchenzentrum

At first glance this 2005 church looks like a Silicon Valley HQ but closer inspection reveals its sensuous design. Plain white facades contrast with the complex interior. A free-standing bell tower introduces a multilayered arrangement of spaces: patios with trees and fountains, gardens and roof terraces. Architect Florian Nagler calls St Florian a town within a town; we call it an oasis. The use of white, grey and black inside the church creates a warm welcome, enhanced by countless small pendant lights. The highlight is the 120 sq m window (opposite), Europe's biggest glass painting, by Hella De Santarossa. The parish centre is part of the remarkably designed satellite town Messestadt Riem, built on a former airport west of Munich. *Platz der Menschenrechte 1, Messestadt Riem, www.sankt-florian.org*

ZOB

The ultramodern ZOB (central bus station), by local firm Auer + Weber + Assoziierte, is a whale of a building. Handling 36,500 buses and their passengers every year, it needs to be. Its elongated shape, the smart use of materials and the fact it has been elevated saves it from intruding too much on the surrounding landscape. A rib cage comprising 29km of aluminium pipes has an interesting effect on sunny days when it casts a shadow. The structure's overall concept follows that of an airport, with terminals and a non-travel area for retail and catering outlets, mostly inhabited by big chains. The ZOB is also home to the anonymous nightclub Neuraum (T 381 538 999), which mainly attracts twentysomethings.
Arnulfstrasse 21, T 4520 9890,
www.muenchen-zob.de

Fünf Höfe

This European take on a typical American mall stands right in the centre of Munich. The challenge for architects Herzog & De Meuron was to open up a hitherto closed block and integrate it into a historic area. The result is a complex of little alleys, big spaces and five courtyards (*Fünf Höfe*). To emphasise different parts of the structure, contrasting materials were used; rough brick for the Schäfflerhof, glass and steel for the Maffeihof and plaster sequinned with glass for the Prannerpassage. The centrepiece is the Salvatorpassage, covered with hanging plants and lights. Look for the huge sphere by artist Olafur Eliasson. The mall is home to upscale shops and eateries, and the Hypo Kunsthalle (T 224 412), a major art exhibition space. *Kardinal-Faulhaber Strasse 10, T 2444 9580, www.fuenfhoefe.de*

Jüdisches Museum

Completed in 2006, 78 years after the idea was first mooted, the Jewish Museum is a short stroll from Viktualienmarkt of three buildings: a museum, a synagogue and a community centre. To make each entity, travertine was used for the facades, and different finishes gave them their own identity. The rough and rocky cladding of the synagogue references the Wailing Wall, its upper half is vitrified and covered by stylised Stars of David and a bronze-coloured mesh. All three buildings are connected by underground passages. Book a guided tour to get the most out of your visit. Afterwards, enjoy a meal at Munich's only kosher restaurant, Einstein (T 202 400 333), also on St Jakobs-Platz. *St Jakobs-Platz 16, T 2339 6096, www.juedisches-museum-muenchen.de*

Deutsche Bahn Betriebszentrale
This squat, cylindrical, mausoleum-like
rail operations centre, created by local
firm SIAT, sits between a verdigris office
block, a flyover and the railway, yet
still emits a powerful presence. Its
uncompromising black core is swathed
in horizontal, silver-edged blades. The
bunker impression is relieved at night
when glowing lights provide signs of life.
Richelstrasse 3, www.db.de

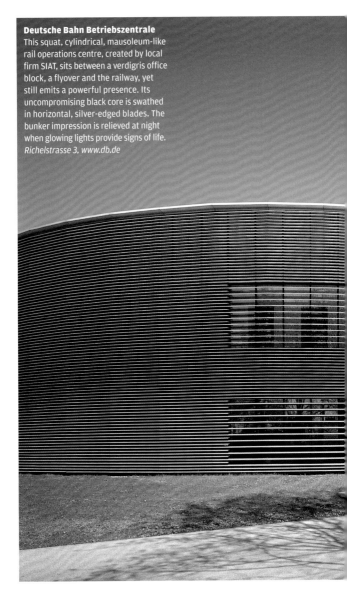

SHOPPING

THE BEST RETAIL THERAPY AND WHAT TO BUY

Steer clear of the crowds and run-of-the-mill high-street brands around Marienplatz and the Rathaus, and head to the Fünf Höfe (see p076) and Maximilianstrasse, where there is more fur than at the zoo, for an urbane shopping experience. The best independent retail is elsewhere, particularly in Glockenbachviertel, where you can find an eclectic mix of products, such as the percussion instruments at Troyan (Klenzestrasse 30, T 267 421). There are also a number of ateliers offering unique pieces. Be it a handmade leather wallet from Antonetty Lederwerkstatt (Klenzestrasse 56, T 269 129) or a blouse by Clara Niggl (Rumfordstrasse 8, T 2602 6035), it's a pleasure to see the results of real craftsmanship.

Stroll north up Leopoldstrasse to the university area for the fashion boutiques and jewellery stores around Türkenstrasse and Hohenzollernstrasse, and myriad interesting shops around Wedekindplatz, including the huge denim selection at Flip Munich (Feilitzschstrasse 4-6, T 3808 8659). In Altstadt, pay a visit to concept store Crooma (Thierschstrasse 23, T 2300 0858) for photo-art, design objects and furniture, and Shu Shu (Neuturmstrasse 2, T 2554 9061), a showroom for handpicked design items from Japan. For a sweet treat, visit tiny Sama Sama (Westenriederstrasse 21, T 2916 3379) and savour the city's most delicately sculptured pralines while sipping a hot chocolate. *For full addresses, see Resources.*

Soda

When Sebastian Steinacker moved back to Munich from London he felt his home city was lacking a design-led bookshop comparable to those in the English capital. Acting on this, he opened Soda, which offers an outstanding and regularly updated selection of handpicked tomes and magazines covering art, design and fashion, including some rare gems such as Japanese lifestyle review *Free & Easy*.

Despite the workshop-style interiors with high ceilings, white walls and dark flooring, Steinacker has created a welcoming atmosphere, which makes flicking through his books a real pleasure. Check the website for details of book launches, where you can mingle with the leading lights of Munich's growing design scene. *Rumfordstrasse 3, T 2024 5353, www.sodabooks.com*

Ingo Maurer
Follow the orange birds to find Maurer's
lighting showroom in a Schwabing
backyard. He 'planted' the birds in the
trees to brighten up a gloomy winter's
day. Maurer's store has more than
100 products, prototypes, one-offs and
design models that highlight his passion
for illumination and beautiful design.
Kaiserstrasse 47, T 381 6060,
www.ingo-maurer.com

Talbot Runhof

Johnny Talbot and Adrian Runhof produce luxurious women's evening- and partywear, which includes signature stretch-taffeta dresses. 'We aim for a modern approach to party dressing,' says Runhof. 'It's more casual, with great separates ready to mix into everyday wear but all very sexy.' Also very sexy are the high-gloss, purple and hot orange (or Cointreau in TR speak) interiors by locally based designers Tredup Hamann. A velvet-covered banister leads up to shimmering organza curtains and formalwear. The store has a creative, studio atmosphere, changing rooms are spacious, and the chillout gallery space, with crystal beads and suspended day beds, provides a welcome respite for male hangers-on.
Klenzestrasse 41, T 236 6730, www.talbotrunhof.com

Menu 12

'Fashion and lifestyle concept store' is only a skin-deep description of Menu 12. Having worked in fashion for years, owner Carolin Schuster-Böckler has created her own vision of what the shopping experience should be, and it's one that inspires on every visit. Everything within the store is movable and for sale so the space never looks the same twice. Explore a variety of exclusive fashion labels, objets d'art or accessories. The owner's latest findings may even include one-off antique furniture pieces, such as a 19th-century divan with antlers. Schuster-Böckler is constantly looking to extend the range: her next coup is a bespoke tailoring service in collaboration with a Savile Row-trained tailor.
Reichenbachstrasse 12, T 2422 3513, www.menu12.com

Patrik Muff

Located on the edge of Altstadt, Patrik Muff's shop may take a little tracking down, and once inside it seems that the jewellery-designing artisan has done some hunting of his own, as deer antlers decorate the walls. In reality more gatherer than hunter, Muff's solid sterling silver and gold jewellery – heavy in both imagery and weight – is displayed in collector's-style glass cabinets. His inspiration is varied, embracing the natural world and the sacred symbols of Buddhist iconography. Having trained as a goldsmith, Muff works with traditional techniques and materials. Clients range from Munich's well-to-do to the city's alternative set, and he's even designed a line for 260-year-old porcelain firm Nymphenburg. Bespoke commissions are by appointment at Muff's workshop. *Frauenstrasse 15, T 123 7040, www.patrikmuff.com*

SPORTS AND SPAS
WORK OUT, CHILL OUT OR JUST WATCH

Munich is a mecca for fresh-air fiends, with lakes and pools, such as Dantebad (see p090) and the refurbished Südbad (Valleystrasse 37, T 2361 5050), seemingly round every corner. Designated bicycle paths on most streets, coupled with careful drivers, means that cycling is the most enjoyable way to get around; the bike-share scheme Nextbike (www.nextbike.de) has more than 30 stations. Much of this sport-loving city is given over to recreation, and forests, rivers and mountains are all within striking distance for the adventurous visitor. Add a stable Continental climate (although it can get very cold) with plenty of bright days, and you have every reason to leave your hotel bar. Those with wetsuits can even go surfing in the centre of the city: the Eisbach is a narrow tributary of the Isar that forms a permanent wave as it races out from under Prinzregentenstrasse, between Haus der Kunst (see p062) and Bayerisches National Museum (T 211 2401). On winter nights, the obsessed bring a generator and floodlights.

The city is full of tanning shops and hair stylists, so the slow pick-up of the day spa phenomenon comes as a surprise. Apart from those in the luxury hotels, such as Andrée Putman's Blue Spa in the Bayerischer Hof (see p016), with its wood-trim lockers, subtle nautical theme and retractable roof over the raised pool, try Just Pure (see p092) for some serious sanctuary.

For full addresses, see Resources.

Schuster

Those inspired by Munich's mountain scenery come to Schuster to get kitted out for the high life. The family-owned retailer, which celebrates its centenary in 2013, supplies gear for most mountain sports and also caters for cyclists and runners. Among the 500 brands stocked are several market leaders that are designed and often made in Germany, including Völkl skis, Meindl boots, Deuter backpacks and Bogner clothing. A team of knowledgeable staff offers sage advice and helps with finding and fitting the right kit. Skis and bindings can also be serviced here. But the feature that sets Schuster apart is an indoor five-storey climbing wall, with routes of varying difficulty, on which to try gear and hone your moves. *Rosenstrasse 1-5, T 237 070, www.sport-schuster.de*

Dantebad

This 50m stainless-steel outdoor pool
is the best in town. Open all year round,
it's well heated, and on a winter's night
the steam following each swimmer is a
surreal sight. There's an adjacent 'wellness'
pool, with state-of-the-art hydro-technics,
and in summer you can take your pick
of Dantebad's three other 50m lap pools
or, if you're feeling buff, the nudity area.
Postillonstrasse 17, T 2361 5050

Just Pure Day Spa

The beauty products created by Gabriela Just are not only produced in Germany from wholly natural ingredients but also in accordance with the phases of the moon. The complete range is available in Just's flagship store in Herzog & de Meuron's Fünf Höfe shopping complex (see p076), where express treatments are also available. If you have more time, experience the full massage and beauty programme in the all-white interiors of this spa in Schwabing, a contributor to the gentrification of Wedekindplatz. A short walk away is the stylish beauty salon, Wax in the City (T 3888 7088), which does exactly what it says on the tin, and to complete the package, the flotation centre Float (T 3303 9699) is round the corner. *Siegesstrasse 13, T 3835 6999, www.justpure.com*

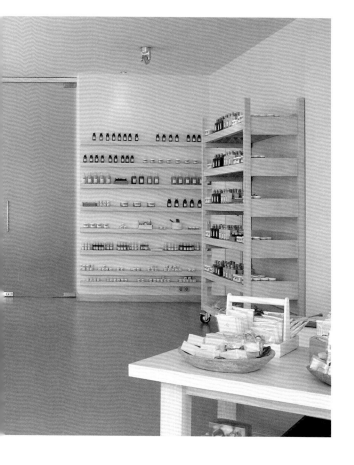

Airyoga
Swiss architect Damir Masek's interiors
blend matte wood, steel and concrete
with energising blood-red ochre fabrics.
Balinese furnishings, and yoga wear
designed by owner Dagmar Stuhr, add
a softer touch. The industrial-style main
room (pictured) is lit from the floor to
evoke dawn – the best time for yoga.
*1st floor, Schrannenhalle, Blumenstrasse
6, T 2322 5930, www.airyoga.com*

ESCAPES

WHERE TO GO IF YOU WANT TO LEAVE TOWN

Despite the attractions of Munich's extensive parks and gardens, an escape from the city is sometimes necessary. Most of the action is to the south, where lakes, such as Starnberger See (see p098), or Walchensee, where the water is clean enough to drink, beckon in the summer. Only a short distance away, the snow-capped peaks of Garmisch-Partenkirchen await skiers, though not all will have the nerve to launch from its impressive jump (see p100). Mountain towns strung along the Alps – Brauneck-Lenggries, Spitzingsee and Sudelfeld-Bayrischzell – are within striking distance of Munich and linked by a common ski pass. In summer be sure to pack a pair of hiking boots or cycling shoes.

The area's beauty attracted the eccentric King Ludwig II, whose deluded obsession with building magnificent castles, such as Neuschwanstein (T 83 6293 9880), bankrupted his kingdom. It was also attractive to the artists of the early 20th century who joined the celebrated *Blaue Reiter* (Blue Rider) group of Wassily Kandinsky and Franz Marc in Murnau am Staffelsee to the south-west. Summer in Munich wouldn't be complete without sipping a cold *Mass* (litre) of the gold stuff in a *Biergarten* under the chestnut trees. They get busy in the centre, so take a short trip along the Isar to Flaucher island. Also close to the city are the sumptuous palace and follies of Schloss Nymphenburg (opposite). *For full addresses, see Resources.*

Schloss Nymphenburg

Although it's roughly half the size of the Englischer Garten, the park at Schloss Nymphenburg is still large enough for the visitor to find tranquillity among the Versailles-style gardens and ponds behind the fairytale Italianate palace. The woods and meadows feature incredible rococo hunting lodges and follies, including one of Europe's first tiled and heated indoor pools. The main baroque palace has a variety of grand staterooms and King Ludwig I's famous 'Gallery of Beauties'. Adjacent is the orangery, which hosts occasional art exhibitions, and in front of the palace is a group of buildings where Nymphenburg porcelain is produced.
T 179 080, www.schloesser.bayern.de

Buchheim Museum, Bernried
A multitude of crystal-clear lakes fans
out in a loose arc to the south of Munich.
Starnberger See is one of the closest
and offers the added attraction of
the Buchheim Museum's expressionist
art collection. Don't miss Tegernsee
either – a beautiful, narrow stretch of
water on the panoramic Alpenstrasse.
*Hirschgarten 1, T 815 899 7020,
www.buchheimmuseum.de*

Garmisch-Partenkirchen
An hour's drive south-west of Munich,
where the Alps rise from Bavarian
pastures, Garmisch-Partenkirchen is a
town dedicated to Alpine sports, winter
and summer. Since 2008, it has been
graced by Loenhart & Mayr's award-
winning ski jump. The cantilevered
structure is illuminated at night, and
becomes visible along the valley.
www.gapa.de

Schloss Elmau

It might rack up some big numbers – 130 bedrooms, six restaurants (one with a Michelin star), four spas, three lounges, two libraries, a concert hall and a bookshop – but despite its size, Schloss Elmau feels chalet-like and quirky. This is not only because of its Alpine surroundings but also its history. It was built in 1916 by writer Johannes Müller as a sanctuary for his intellectual guests. Grandson Dietmar Müller-Elmau has pursued the idea, creating a beautiful, family-friendly hotel that is also a superb venue for concerts, talks and other cultural events. Of the outdoor activities, guided walking tours, with a mountain hut stopover and bathing at Lake Ferchensee, are popular. *Elmau, T 0882 3180, www.schloss-elmau.de*

NOTES

SKETCHES AND MEMOS

RESOURCES
CITY GUIDE DIRECTORY

HOTELS
ADDRESSES AND ROOM RATES

Anna Hotel 020
  Room rates:
  double, from €220;
  Room 003, €400;
  Tower Suite, €600
  Schützenstrasse 1
  T 599 940
  www.annahotel.de
Bayerischer Hof 016
  Room rates:
  double, €345
  Promenadeplatz 2-6
  T 21 200
  www.bayerischerhof.de
The Charles Hotel 016
  Room rates:
  double, from €270
  Sophienstrasse 28
  T 544 5550
  www.charleshotel.de
Cortiina 022
  Room rates:
  double, from €139;
  Business Suite, €465
  Ledererstrasse 8
  T 242 2490
  www.cortiina.de
Hotel Königshof 016
  Room rates:
  double, from €350
  Karlsplatz 25
  T 551 360
  www.koenigshof-muenchen.de

Louis Hotel 017
  Room rates:
  double, from €175;
  Market Room, €309;
  Louis Room, €450
  Viktualienmarkt 6
  T 4111 9080
  www.louis-hotel.com
La Maison 030
  Room rates:
  double, €180;
  Double Light Room, €180;
  Room 104, €200
  Occamstrasse 24
  T 3303 5550
  www.hotel-la-maison.com
H'Otello Advokat B'01 028
  Room rates:
  double, from €155;
  Standard Single, €135
  Baaderstrasse 1
  T 4583 1200
  www.hotel-advokat.de
Ritzi 027
  Room rates:
  double, from €149;
  Surf Room, €179;
  Indonesian Room, €179;
  Red Room, €209
  Maria-Theresia-Strasse 2a
  T 414 240 890
  www.hotel-ritzi.de
Schloss Elmau 102
  Room rates:
  double, from €409
  Elmau
  T 0882 3180
  www.schloss-elmau.de

Sheraton Arabellapark
Room rates:
double, from €99
Arabellastrasse 5
T 92 320
www.sheraton.com/bogenhausen
Sofitel Bayerpost
Room rates:
double, from €200;
Duplex Suite, €615
Bayerstrasse 12
T 599 480
www.sofitel.com
Hotel Vier Jahreszeiten Kempinski
Room rates:
double, from €260
Maximilianstrasse 17
T 2125 2799
www.kempinski-vierjahreszeiten.de

WALLPAPER* CITY GUIDES

Executive Editor
Rachael Moloney

Editor
Robin Barton
Authors
Guy Dittrich
Viola Reise

Art Director
Loran Stosskopf
Art Editor
Eriko Shimazaki
Designer
Mayumi Hashimoto
Map Illustrator
Russell Bell

Photography Editor
Sophie Corben
Deputy Photography Editor
Anika Burgess
Photography Assistant
Nabil Butt

Chief Sub-Editor
Nick Mee
Sub-Editor
Emily Brooks

Editorial Assistant
Emma Harrison

Intern
Franziska Hensel

Wallpaper* Group Editor-in-Chief
Tony Chambers
Publishing Director
Gord Ray
Managing Editor
Jessica Diamond

Contributor
Bart van Poll

Wallpaper* ® is a registered trademark of IPC Media Limited

First published 2007
Second edition (revised and updated) 2012
Reprinted 2014

All prices are correct at the time of going to press, but are subject to change.

Printed in China

PHAIDON

Phaidon Press Limited
Regent's Wharf
All Saints Street
London N1 9PA

Phaidon Press Inc
180 Varick Street
New York, NY 10014

Phaidon® is a registered trademark of Phaidon Press Limited

www.phaidon.com

A CIP Catalogue record for this book is available from the British Library.

ISBN 978 0 7148 6659 8

PHOTOGRAPHERS

AllOver Photography/ Alamy
Buchheim Museum, pp098-099

Bora/Alamy
Schloss Nymphenburg, p097

Goodshoot/Corbis
Munich city view, inside front cover

Massimo Listri/Corbis
Residenz, p034

Florian Monheim/ Bildarchiv Monheim/ Fotofinder
Chinesischer Turm, p033

Roland Halbe
Allianz Arena, p068
Herz Jesu Kirche, p069

Hubertus Hamm
Garmisch-Partenkirchen, pp100-101

Nagib Khazaka
BMW Headquarters, pp010-011
Louis Hotel, p017, pp018-019
Alpentraum, p035
Heart, pp038-039
Gesellschaftsraum, p041
Edmoses, pp042-043
Goldene Bar, pp046-047
La Baracca, p050, p051
Glockenbach, pp052-053
P1, p054
Röcklplatz, p055
L'Osteria Künstlerhaus, p057
Hanoi, pp058-059
Benedikt Sarreiter, p063
Museum Brandhorst, p065
St Florian Kirchenzentrum, p072, p073
ZOB, pp074-075
Fünf Höfe, p076
Jüdisches Museum, p077
Soda, p081
Ingo Maurer, pp082-083
Menu 12, p085
Patrik Muff, pp086-087

Duccio Malagamba
BMW Welt, pp066-067

Simone Rosenberg
HypoVereinsbank HQ, p012
Olympic Tower, p013

Mercedes Building, pp014-015
Cortiina, p022, p023
Ritzi, p027
H'Otello Advokat B'01, pp028-029
La Maison, p030, p031
Vinaiolo, p044
Eisbach Bar & Küche, p045
Brenner, p049
Trachtenvogl, p056
Wirtshaus in der Au, p060
Akademie der Bildenden Künste, pp070-071
Deutsche Bahn Betriebszentrale, pp078-079
Talbot Runhof, p084
Schuster, p089
Dantebad, pp090-091
Just Pure Day Spa, pp092-093

MUNICH
A COLOUR-CODED GUIDE TO THE HOT 'HOODS

ALTSTADT/LEHEL
Beneath the Frauenkirche's twin spires lie a maze of streets and upscale stores

MAXVORSTADT
The Kunstareal art hub and Pinakothek museums stand at the city's cultural heart

GLOCKENBACHVIERTEL
Packed with ateliers, the artists' quarter is where you'll find cutting-edge design

SCHWABING
University buildings, the Olympic complex and parks comprise this vast northern quarter

HAIDHAUSEN
The action is centred on Wiener Platz market square in this upwardly mobile district

BOGENHAUSEN
Villas nestle among the Isar's forested flanks, with Arabella Park's towers to the north

For a full description of each neighbourhood, see the Introduction.
Featured venues are colour-coded, according to the district in which they are located.